# Fall in Love with Me

Love Letters from Jesus

Jim Branch

*For Cannon, who is teaching me how to fall in love in a whole new way.*

Cover image is public domain in its country of origin and other countries where the copyright term is the author's life plus 80 years or fewer. It is public domain in the United States because it was published (or registered with the U. S. Copyright office) before January 1, 1926.

# Introduction

*"We love because he first loved us,"* (1 John 4:19) not vice versa. Therefore, love always starts with God. Our love for him can only be a reflection of, and a response to, his great love for us. It follows that if we want to grow in our love for God, we must continually be captured by his passionate love for us. We must be seized by the power of his great affection.

How does that happen? Only through knowing him better and better. It happens through sitting in his presence and enjoying his company, through experiencing his embrace and hearing his whispers of delight. Romance takes time and space. In fact, the main reason romances fail is because of the lack of making room for them to grow and flourish. It takes both attention and intention. Affection can do nothing but grow when we are committed to looking deeply into the eyes of our Beloved. When we see the love in his eyes, it kindles the fire of love in our own.

Which brings us to this book. It is simply an invitation to fall more in love with God and to hear his voice through the life and words of Jesus in the most intimate and personal way. For I am convinced that if we read the words of the Scriptures as they were intended, as a love letter from Jesus, it will change everything about us. Because what Jesus is saying to each of us through the Scriptures is not so much "Get your act together," but, "Fall in love with me."

That is my deepest hope for you as you read this book. So take it slow and savor it; do just one letter a day. Read the words of the Scriptures several times, listening to whatever God might have to say to you. Enjoy the reflections and take the time to write Jesus a letter in return. Hopefully, by the end of our journey together, you will be more in love with Jesus than you were when we began. Blessings.

JB

# Letter One

## Listen

In the beginning was the Word, and the Word was with God, and the Word was God. He was with God in the beginning.

Through him all things were made, without him nothing was made that has been made. In him was life, and that life was the light of men. The light shines in the darkness, and the darkness has not overcome it. ~John 1:1-5

## Reflect

My Beloved,

In the beginning, I existed — Father, Son, and Spirit — in an endless dance of passionate love. Intimacy beyond imagination or description. In fact, I was so full of love that I simply couldn't contain myself — I created. That's how you came along. You were not some cosmic accident, but a direct expression of the delights of Divine intimacy. You were created as a result of the affection of the Trinity, in order to be invited into that eternal embrace of love. Always remember that about yourself; it will help you as you try to navigate this life. It will assure you that your identity is a given; it cannot be earned, manufactured, or achieved. And it cannot be lost. You are mine and I made you for love. I made you for myself. Fall in love with me.

> Love,
> Jesus

## Respond

Write a letter to Jesus, telling him all that is in your heart.

# Letter Two

## Listen

There came a man who was sent from God; his name was John. He came as a witness to testify concerning the light, so that through him all men might believe. He himself was not the light; he came only as a witness to the light. The true light that gives light to every man was coming into the world. ~John 1:6-9

## Reflect

My Beloved,

I know it is easy, in this noisy and chaotic world, to forget who you are and to forget who I am. The voices within and without are loud indeed. But don't worry, I didn't leave you alone. I love you so much that I sent people to you, in order to remind you of the truth. John was one of those, and there are plenty more. In fact, don't be surprised if I send you one today. Oh, you might be too busy, or too consumed, to notice, but they are there, and they are sent.

Just stop for a minute. Think about all of the people throughout the course of your lifetime that I have sent to you. They are many. Let them be a reminder to you that I love you, and I have not forgotten about you. And just as I have sent these people to you, so you are sent to others. Love them the way I have loved you, it's one of my favorite ways to wrap my arms around those I love.

So fall in love with me, Beloved, and go love others as a result.

Love,
Jesus

# Respond

Write a letter to Jesus, telling him all that is in your heart.

# Letter Three

## Listen

He was in the world, and though the world was made through him, the world did not recognize him. He came to that which was his own, but his own did not receive him. Yet to all who received him, to those who believed in his name, he gave the right to become children of God—children born not of natural descent, nor a husband's will, but born of God. ~John 1:10-13

## Reflect

My Beloved,

Believe it or not, my deepest desire is for you to become all that I dreamt you to be when you were woven together in the depths of the earth. (Psalm 139:15) And the way you do that is by recognizing my love, believing it's really true, receiving it into the core of your being, and letting it take hold of you as you become a beloved child of mine. Allow my love to transform your heart and soul, for you cannot do it on your own. You cannot change yourself; you've tried that over and over again. You cannot behave your way into love, you can only love your way into behavior. It is the recognizing, believing, and receiving of my unfailing love that brings about this becoming. It is not a product that can be manufactured, but a fruit that must be grown.

So fall in love with me, my little one, and let me be the one who captures your heart and forms your life.

Love,<br>
Jesus

# Respond

Write a letter to Jesus, telling him all that is in your heart.

# Letter Four

## Listen

The Word became flesh and made his dwelling among us. We have seen his glory, the glory of the One and Only, who came from the Father, full of grace and truth. ~John 1:14

## Reflect

My Beloved,

I just can't stay away from you; the drive of my love is just too strong. I think about you all the time. I sing over you as you sleep. I can't hold back my hands from your hair or my lips from your cheeks. There is no distance too far, no valley too deep, no cost too high, and no price too great. Nothing can keep me away from you.

You look at yourself and see only your sin, but I don't see your sin at all. It has been removed from my sight, as far as the east is from the west. I have twisted my mouth to fit your crooked lips, just to show you that our kiss still works. I have made you pure and clean and whole and new. I see only your beauty.

So fall in love with me, my love, for I cannot resist you.

Love,<br>
Jesus

## Respond

Write a letter to Jesus, telling him all that is in your heart.

# Letter Five

## Listen

For from his fullness we have all received grace upon grace. For the law was given through Moses; grace and truth came through Jesus Christ. No one has ever seen God; but God the One and Only, who is at the Father's side, has made him known. ~John 1:16-18

## Reflect

My Beloved,

Most people in this world will never — and can never — love you enough to give you both grace and truth. They will always err on one side or the other. But not me, I will always give you both — in perfect harmony. You see, to me they are not two different things, but two parts of one incredibly beautiful whole. For grace without truth has no backbone, no power, no direction; and truth without grace has no kindness, no compassion, no heart. So rest assured, I will always give you both.

I will always show you grace by telling you how wonderful you are and how delighted I am with you. But I will not stop there, I will also tell you when you are living in a way that is less than what I desire for you. The three main enemies of your soul — the world, the flesh, and the devil — will constantly try to make you believe things that are simply not true. But don't worry, if you listen to me, I will tell you when you are believing lies, not seeing things clearly, or straying from me and my word. I will tell you when you are buying into the world's mindset, rather than seeking my heart and mind. I will tell you when you are being seduced into believing things about yourself and your world that are simply not true. I will tell you when you are not being your best, made-in-the-image-of-God self. Because I have big dreams for you, even bigger than those you have for yourself. And I do not want you to settle for less. That's what it means to be full of grace and truth.

My Father is like that too. Part of the reason I came to earth in the first place was to reveal his heart to you. And his heart is full of grace and truth, just like mine. Always remember that.

Fall in love with me.

                                                Love,
                                                Jesus

## Respond

Write a letter to Jesus, telling him all that is in your heart.

# Letter Six

## Listen

And this is the testimony of John, when the Jews sent priests and Levites from Jerusalem to ask him, "Who are you?" He confessed, and did not deny, but confessed, "I am not the Christ." And they asked him, "What then? Are you Elijah?" He said, "I am not." "Are you the Prophet?" And he answered, "No." So they said to him, "Who are you? We need to give an answer to those who sent us. What do you say about yourself?" He said, "I am the voice of one crying out in the wilderness, 'Make straight the way of the Lord,' as the prophet Isaiah said." ~John 1:19-23

## Reflect

My Beloved,

Long before the day you were born, I was already at work *making a way* in you. And until the day you pass from this life to the next, I will still be *making a way* in you. You see, I love you so much that I am fully committed to your becoming. Oh, not just becoming who and what you want to be, that would be short-sighted, but becoming who and what I made you to be.

If you look back, you are likely to see it. If you look around right now, you are still likely to notice it. And as you look ahead, you may be confident that it will continue. The people and places and events of this life—both the most profound and the most painful—have all been a part of this process, a part of me *making a way* in you. Believe it or not, there has always been an intent of God behind the content of your life. And that intent is to show you how deeply you are loved and adored.

In your moments of deepest joy, I have been *making a way* in you. And in you moments of unbearable pain, I have been *making a way* in you.  You might not have been able to see it or feel it at that moment, but I was right there with you, carrying you along, wiping your tears, and comforting your broken heart.  That is how much I love you.

And the way I have been *making in you* is also the way straight into my heart.  Follow it and you will find me, as well as all of your deepest hopes and wildest dreams.  Fall in love with me.

Love,<br>Jesus

## Respond

Write a letter to Jesus, telling him all that is in your heart.

# Letter Seven

## Listen

The next day John saw Jesus coming toward him and said, "Look, the Lamb of God, who takes away the sin of the world! This is the one I meant when I said, 'A man who comes after me has surpassed me because he was before me.' I myself did not know him, but the reason I came was that he might be revealed to Israel." ~John 1:29-31

## Reflect

My Beloved,

Before the foundations of the world were set into place, you were the object of my love and affection. Before anything else existed, my Father and I dreamt together about how we could show you our love in the most extravagant way possible. So from the very beginning we decided that I, the Alpha and the Omega, the Beginning and the End, the King of Kings and Lord of Lords, would also be the Lamb of God, who takes away the sin of the world.

You see, sin did not take us by surprise; it did not catch us off guard. We knew full well the reality and the gravity of your choice. We knew the full implications of the Fall, and planned all along to use it in order to show you the full extent of our love, at the cross. Thus, my being the Lamb of God was not merely a knee-jerk reaction to sin, but the sovereign intention of Divine Love. All those lambs, for all those years, pointed forward to me, the one true Lamb of God, who actually could take away the sin of the world. And it brought me great delight to do so. The Father and I wanted to show you the full extent of our love, so I voluntarily took all of your sin upon myself. I did this so that you might be whole and free and forgiven. So that we could live together in intimacy and passionate union for all eternity.

More than anything I just want you to know, beyond a shadow of a doubt, that you are fully and deeply and unconditionally loved. And hopefully, as a result, you might fall more in love with me.

> Love,
> Jesus

## Respond

Write a letter to Jesus, telling him all that is in your heart.

# Letter Eight

## Listen

The next day John was there again with two of his disciples. When he saw Jesus passing by, he said, "Look, the Lamb of God!"

When the two disciples heard him say this, they followed Jesus. Turing around, Jesus saw them following and asked, "What do you want?"

They said, "Rabbi" (which means Teacher), "where are you staying?"

"Come," he replied, "and you will see."

So they went and saw where he was staying, and spent that day with him. ~John 1:35-39

## Reflect

My Beloved,

What do you want? I mean, what do you really want? Do you even know? Do you want to be truly seen? Do you want to be deeply known? Do you want to be passionately loved? These are questions that you must answer, for *your feet will always move in the direction of what you really want*. Or, at least, in the direction of what you think you want.

But sometimes you stop too near the surface in answering that question. Sometimes you settle for happy, when you could have joyful. Sometimes you settle for easy, when it is difficulty that produces the most fruit in your life. Sometimes you settle for safety, when it is passion and adventure you really long for. So let me ask you again, what do you really want in the deepest parts of your heart and soul?

I see you. I really see you. Otherwise, I would never have asked you the question in the first place. I know you. I really know you. I know how, and for whom, you were made. And I love you. I really love you, more than you can ever ask or imagine. In fact, I care enough about you to ask you the question, "What do you want?" Ultimately, it is a question that will always lead you to me, for I am the deepest desire of your heart and you are the deepest desire of mine. So fall in love with me, my Beloved.

Love,<br>Jesus

## Respond

Write a letter to Jesus, telling him all that is in your heart.

# Letter Nine

## Listen

Andrew, Simon Peter's brother, was one of the two who heard what John had said and who had followed Jesus. The first thing Andrew did was to find his brother Simon and tell him, "We have found the Messiah" (that is, the Christ). And he brought him to Jesus.

Jesus looked at him and said, "You are Simon, son of John. You will be called Cephas" (which, when translated, is Peter). ~John 1:40-42

## Reflect

My Beloved,

I know how hard it is trying to figure out who you are in this crazy world; it can be very confusing. There are so many voices, both within and around you, trying to get your attention; each claiming to have the truth. But I am the only one who can tell you who you really are, for I made you. Therefore, listen closely to me.

You will be tempted to believe that you are what you *do*, but that is not the truth. Your identity is not something you can create, conjure, contrive, achieve, or manufacture; it can only be bestowed. It can only be given to you by the One who made you.

And you will be tempted to try to discern who you are by what has worked for you thus far in your life, by what has gotten you the most praise, affirmation, attention, affection, or adoration from those around you. This is incredibly shaky ground upon which to build an identity. It is not who you really are, but merely who you have become as a result of your needy grasping for worth and value. Being more outgoing, for example, may just be the result of that need; while being more reserved may just be a fear-based strategy for safety and security. Many of your traits and patterns have been learned and adopted through pain and brokenness, as well as through performance and manipulation. They are not really who you are, but only who you have become as a result of what has "worked" for you thus far. Which means that some of the things that feel most authentic to you might just be your misguided interpretations of the ebb and flow of your life's events—both its pains and its successes. Never forget, my Beloved, that, *"the heart is deceitful above all things and beyond cure. Who can understand it?"* (Jer. 17:9)

That's why you have to listen carefully to me; I will show you who you really are, the same way I did Simon Peter. I have a name picked out for you that no one else knows anything about. It is what I called you when I breathed you into being, and what I will call you again when you enter into glory. (Rev.2:17) It is my pet name for you. It is a name of love and delight. It is a name that tells you who I made you to be. I can hardly wait to share it with you. I love you so much, my Beloved; fall in love with me.

Love,<br>Jesus

## Respond

Write a letter to Jesus, telling him all that is in your heart.

# Letter Ten

## Listen

When Jesus saw Nathanael approaching, he said of him, "Here is a true Israelite, in whom there is nothing false."

"How do you know me?" Nathanael asked.

Jesus answered, "I saw you while you were still under the fig tree before Philip called you."

The Nathanael declared, "Rabbi, you are the Son of God; you are the King of Israel."

Jesus said, "You believe because I told you I saw you under the fig tree. You shall see greater things than that. I tell you the truth, you shall see heaven open, and the angels of God ascending and descending on the Son of Man." ~John 1:47-51

## Reflect

My Beloved,

I know that, at times, it can feel like no one really sees you, like no one really knows you. I know that it can feel like no one really understands what's going on in the depths of your heart and soul. Trust me, I know how incredibly lonely that can be.

But fear not, I see you. And I don't mean that I see only the worst parts of you, the parts you try to hide from yourself and your world. The fact is that I see the very best parts of you as well. I see the beautiful truth in you that no one else sees; the truth that has been covered over by brokenness and dysfunction and sin. And that beauty is the part I desire to call out in you. I want to speak my truth and my love into your deepest fears, and bring you to life once again.

That's how much I love you, Beloved, so fall in love with me.

> Love,
> Jesus

## Respond

Write a letter to Jesus, telling him all that is in your heart.

# Letter Eleven

## Listen

Nearby stood six stone water jars, the kind used by the Jews for ceremonial washing, each holding from twenty to thirty gallons.

Jesus said to the servants, "Fill the jars with water"; so they filled them to the brim. Then he told them, "Now draw some out and take it to the master of the banquet."

They did so, and the master of the banquet tasted the water that had been turned into wine. He did not realize where it had come from, though the servants who had drawn the water knew. Then he called the bridegroom aside and said, "Everyone brings out the choice wine first and then the cheaper wine after the guests have had too much to drink; but you have saved the best till now."

This, the first of his miraculous signs, Jesus performed at Cana in Galilee. He thus revealed his glory, and his disciples put their faith in him. ~John 2:6-11

## Reflect

My Beloved,

My love is like fine wine, it is full and rich and robust and intoxicating. And because it is so wonderfully deep and alive and complex, it can go unappreciated by those who are not paying attention, by those whose palates are unrefined, by those who are used to drinking the "cheap stuff" of this world.

You see, my love is not just any old wine, it is the best of wines. And until you have tasted my love, everything else is bland and lifeless and shallow and unsatisfying in comparison. But how will you ever know that if you have never fully tasted and savored it? How can you ever know real love if you have just settled for cheap imitations? Once you have tasted the passion and the extravagance and the goodness of my love, nothing else in this world can ever fully satisfy. And once you have finally started to live out of my abundance, rather than living out of scarcity, you can actually begin to offer that abundance to others. It's what you were made for. Others will actually be able taste my abundance in you.

Just as I wanted for my friends in Cana, I also want the best for you. I don't want you to settle for less than what I made you for. Only the best wine will do for our wedding feast, and my love is deeper and richer and more satisfying than the best of wines.

In fact, my deepest hope is that one day you will know my love so well that you will be able to say: "Let him kiss me with the kisses of his mouth — for your love is more delightful than wine." (Song of Songs 1:2) So fall in love with me, my Beloved, for I am crazy-in-love with you.

Love,<br>
Jesus

## Respond

Write a letter to Jesus, telling him all that is in your heart.

# Letter Twelve

# Listen

When it was almost time for the Jewish Passover, Jesus went up to Jerusalem. In the temple courts he found men selling cattle, sheep, and doves, and others sitting at tables exchanging money. So he made a whip out of cords, and drove all from the temple area, both sheep and cattle; he scattered the coins of the money changers and overturned their tables. To those who sold doves he said, "Get these out of here! How dare you turn my Father's house into a market!"

His disciples remembered that it is written: "Zeal for your house will consume me." ~John 2:13-17

# Reflect

My Beloved,

Some say that God does not get mad anymore. To be honest, I'm not really sure where they came up with that idea. I guess maybe it makes them feel a little better about the things in their lives (and their world) that are not what I intended them to be.

The truth is that a God who loves, must get mad. The two go hand-in-hand; one cannot be separated from the other. I mean, what kind of God doesn't get mad when those he loves are wounded, mistreated, abused, oppressed, or taken advantage of? What kind of God would that be? And what kind of God doesn't get upset when the people he made to live in intimate union with himself are settling for so much less than that? What kind of God does not want more for his beloved creation? You'd better hope I still get mad, otherwise you are all in for a world full of disappointment and pain, with no one to pursue, protect, defend, or fight for you.

How would you feel if I just stood by and did nothing while all of those poor worshippers at the temple in Jerusalem were being taken advantage of in the name of religion? They needed someone to be their advocate, their defender, their King, their Savior. That's why I couldn't just stand by and watch it happen; I had to do something. I had to do something for them and I have to do something for you.

Take heart, I know it looks like a lot of terrible and tragic things go on in this world, while I stand by and do nothing. But know this; I will do something. I will be with you in the midst of your suffering and pain, and one day I will intervene. One day I will come and redeem it all. I will come again and turn over the tables of all who wound and hurt and oppress. What kind of God would I be if I didn't?

I love you, my Beloved, so fall in love with me.

Love,<br>Jesus

## Respond

Write a letter to Jesus, telling him all that is in your heart.

# Letter Thirteen

# Listen

Now while he was in Jerusalem at the Passover Feast, many people saw the miracles he was doing and believed in his name. But Jesus would not entrust himself to them, for he knew all men. He did not need man's testimony about man, for he knew what was in a man.

Now there was a man of the Pharisees named Nicodemus, a member of the Jewish ruling council. He came to Jesus at night and said, "Rabbi, we know you are a teacher who has come from God. For no one could perform the miraculous signs you are doing if God were not with him."

In reply, Jesus declared, "I tell you the truth, no one can see the kingdom of God unless he is born again." ~John 2:23-3:3

# Reflect

My Beloved,

Always remember that there can be no birth without conception, and my deepest desire is to conceive my very life within you. It is how you are born again—and again and again. The fact that conception always precedes new birth is an often overlooked part of this eternal mystery. Conception provides the substance and the passion and the intimacy for the life of faith. It is a life of love that I desire, not a life of heartless duty. You see, life with me always starts with romance.

Ultimately, that's what Nicodemus came looking for on that dark evening. His life and his faith had come up short; there was no passion, no intimacy, no romance. And it is impossible to have a relationship with me without romance, though many have tried.

Oh sure, you can try to skip ahead to being "born again" if you want to, but it will leave you lifeless and flat. You were created for so much more than that. You were created out of the depths of divine intimacy, and it is to the depths of divine intimacy you must return.

John of the Cross knew exactly what I'm talking about, when he wrote: "O living flame of love that tenderly wounds my soul in its deepest center! Since now You are not oppressive, now consummate! If it be Your will: tear through the veil of this sweet encounter!"

That is the kind of passion and intimacy and affection I made you for. And that is the kind of man, or woman, to whom I fully entrust myself. For, ultimately, I'm not looking for robots, I am looking for lovers. So fall in love with me.

Love,<br>Jesus

## Respond

Write a letter to Jesus, telling him all that is in your heart.

# Letter Fourteen

# Listen

"Flesh gives birth to flesh, but the Spirit gives birth to spirit. You should not be surprised at my saying, 'You must be born again.' The wind blows wherever it pleases. You hear its sound but you cannot tell where it comes from or where it is going. So it is with everyone born of the Spirit." ~John 3:5-8

# Reflect

My Beloved,

Always remember, "Flesh gives birth to flesh, and Spirit gives birth to spirit." The nature that you feed is the one that's going to grow. If you devote most of your time and space and energy and attention to the flesh, how can you expect anything other than for the life of the flesh to grow within you? Living that life will make you the worst possible version of yourself—fearful, insecure, self-consumed, controlling, and manipulative. But if you devote most of your time and space and energy and attention to the life of the Spirit, I will grow my very life within you, and it will be a beautiful thing.

Beloved, I have breathed my life-giving breath into you. I have placed within your heart and soul the very life of my Spirit. This breath was meant to intoxicate and animate you. Thus, as you grow and mature in our life together, my Spirit will enable you, more and more, to breathe with my breath, to think with my mind, and to love with my heart.

But be careful in trying to predict or determine or manipulate exactly what that will look like, for the winds of my Spirit are wild and free; they come and go as they please. They cannot be tamed or contained or controlled. All you can do is lift your sails and open yourself completely to its blowing. These winds will take you where I want you to go and help you become who I want you to be, if you do not resist them. They will help you to fall more and more in love with me.

Love,<br>Jesus

## Respond

Write a letter to Jesus, telling him all that is in your heart.

# Letter Fifteen

# Listen

"For God so loved the world that he gave his only Son, that whoever believes in him shall not perish but have eternal life. For God did not send his Son into the world to condemn the world, but to save the world through him. Whoever believes in him is not condemned, but whoever does not believe stands condemned already because he has not believed in the name of God's one and only Son.." ~John 3:16-18

# Reflect

My Beloved,

I know you've heard it all before. In fact, you have heard it so often that it has lost its power in your heart and your life, which makes me incredibly sad. The greatest love story of all time has been reduced to the fodder of signs, slogans, and billboards. It has become nothing more than a catch phrase, a weapon used in order to determine who is *in* and who is *out*. That was never my intention. The story of my coming, and the giving of my life, is meant to be *the* story; the story of my relentless love for you.

You see, I came into the world to save you, not to condemn you. I came into the world to show you how fully and completely and unconditionally you are loved. All that's really necessary in return is for you to believe — to be fully convinced — that it's true, which is far easier said than done. Because you don't really believe you are worthy of being loved like that, especially not by me. I guess it's a good thing that your worthiness does not depend on you, huh? It actually depends on me. That's what unconditional love is all about.

But in order for me to save you, you must be convinced that you really need to be saved. That's where the word *condemnation* comes in—such a hard word. Understanding the devastation of the Fall is essential to being able to comprehend the depths of my love. The Fall took the life I had made for us and shattered it into a million pieces. It's like on the very first night of our honeymoon, you went off and slept with the enemy. As a result, everything was broken beyond repair. But it did not take me by surprise, it was all a part of the grand plan to show you the full extent of my love—even though you already stood condemned. I came and took your condemnation upon myself. I came to save you because you desperately needed saving. I came to save you because I would rather die for you than live without you. That is how much I love you, my Beloved. Fall in love with me.

Love,<br>Jesus

## Respond

Write a letter to Jesus, telling him all that is in your heart.

# Letter Sixteen

# Listen

To this John replied, "A man can receive only what is given him from heaven. You yourselves can testify that I said, 'I am not the Christ but am sent ahead of him.' The bride belongs to the bridegroom. The friend who attends the bridegroom waits and listens for him, and is full of joy when he hears the bridegroom's voice. That joy is mine, and is now complete. He must become greater; I must become less." ~John 3:27-30

# Reflect

My Beloved,

I am the bridegroom and you are my radiant bride. You fill my heart with such love and affection. You are constantly on my mind and in my heart. I simply can't take my eyes off of you. You bring a smile to my lips and a song to my soul. You make my heart soar. I am drunk with love for you.

John the Baptist was a friend of mine. He was sent ahead of me to prepare the way for the two of us to be joined. He was not the bridegroom, but the friend of the bridegroom. His role was to watch and wait and listen for my coming. He knew that you, my beloved bride, belonged to me and not to him. And he did not want to get in the way of that. Therefore, it was his great joy to see the two of us come together. His life was about becoming less, that I might become more—that's simply what love does. Love makes us desire more for the Beloved than we do for ourselves.

You would do well to learn from him and to follow his example, for there are many more who I long to bring into intimate union with myself. Now it is your turn to be John the Baptist. Now it is your turn to help make romance with me a possibility. Show them the way into my heart. Speak to them about the depth and breadth and height of my extravagant love. Tell them what our intimate union means to you. Describe, in detail, the joys and delights of living life with me. How else will they know what they are missing? Find your life and your joy by becoming less, that I might become more. Fall in love with me more and more each day, so that they might do the same.

Love,<br>Jesus

## Respond

Write a letter to Jesus, telling him all that is in your heart.

# Letter Seventeen

## Listen

When a Samaritan woman came to draw water, Jesus said to her, "Will you give me a drink?" (His disciples had gone into town to buy food.)

The Samaritan woman said to him, "You are a Jew and I am a Samaritan woman. How can you ask me for a drink?" (For Jews do not associate with Samaritans.)

Jesus answered, "If you knew the gift of God and who it is that asks you for a drink, you would have asked him and he would have given you living water." ~John 4:7-10

## Reflect

My Beloved,

If you would ask, I would give you the moon. The problem is that you always ask for the wrong things. You ask for so much less than what I long to give. You ask for water, when I long to give you living water. You ask for something to quench your thirsty body, when I offer something to quench your thirsty soul. Why would you not dream big? Why would you not ask more of me? Why would you think I would want anything less for you than the full, rich, abundant life you were created for?

Who knows, maybe this life has worn you down and burned you out to the point where you have simply lost hope. Maybe the disappointments have mounted to the point where you just expect less from life than the life I want for you. That breaks my heart. I am sad to see you settle for so much less than the life I imaged for us in the beginning.

Ask for more, my Beloved! Ask for life. Ask for joy. Ask for hope. Ask for peace. Ask for wholeness. Ask for fullness. Ask for abundance. It's what you were made for, and falling in love with me can give it all to you.

Love,<br>Jesus

## Respond

Write a letter to Jesus, telling him all that is in your heart.

# Letter Eighteen

## Listen

Jesus answered, "Everyone who drinks this water will be thirsty again, but whoever drinks the water I give him will never thirst. Indeed, the water I give him will become in him a spring of water welling up to eternal life."

The woman said to him, "Sir, give me this water so that I won't get thirsty and have to keep coming here to draw water."

He told her, "Go, call your husband and come back."

"I have no husband," she replied.

Jesus said to her, "You are right when you say you have no husband. The fact is, you have had five husbands, and the man you have now is not your husband. What you have said is quite true." ~John 4:13-18

## Reflect

My Beloved,

No one can love you like I can—no matter where you go, no matter what you do. So why do you keep running to other places and other people, when the love you so desperately long for can only be found in me?

You keep trying in vain. How many husbands is that now? And yet, you still find yourself empty and alone. I don't say that to shame you, but to awaken you. I am the Lover you have always dreamt about. I am the only lover who will never leave you wanting for more. Come to me, my Beloved, and experience the love that can fully satisfy all of your deepest longings and all your unfulfilled desires. All other loves are just poor imitations of my love. All other lovers will leave you broken, bitter, and disappointed, but my love will be in you a well of living water, springing up to eternal life. So fall in love with me, my Beloved, and know the overflowing fullness of my love.

Love,<br>Jesus

## Respond

Write a letter to Jesus, telling him all that is in your heart.

# Letter Nineteen

## Listen

And there was a certain royal official whose son lay sick at Capernaum. When this man heard that Jesus had arrived in Galilee from Judea, he went to him and begged him to come and heal his son, who was close to death.

"Unless you people see miraculous signs and wonders," Jesus told him, "you will never believe."

The royal official said, "Sir, come down before my child dies."

Jesus replied, "You may go. Your son will live."

The man took Jesus at his word and departed. While he was still on his way, his servants met him with news that his boy was living. When he inquired as to the time when his son got better, they said to him, "The fever left him yesterday at the seventh hour."

Then the father realized that this was the exact time at which Jesus had said to him, "Your son will live." So he and all his household believed. ~John 4:46-53

## Reflect

My Beloved,

You can always *take me at my word*. You don't ever have to wonder if I will have a change of heart or mind toward you. You don't ever have to doubt if I am willing and able to take care of you. You don't ever have to wonder if I am trustworthy. If I say it, it is true, always.

So when I tell you that you are loved, you can believe it. And when I tell you that I am delighted with you, you can be fully convinced of it. When I tell you that your sins are forgiven, you can count on it. And when I tell you that I will never leave you nor forsake you, you can rest assured that it's true.

I will take care of you, Beloved. Do not allow your heart to be controlled by fear and doubt. For even when your life is turned upside down, even when your circumstances look most dire, and even when things seem dark and desperate, you can always count of me. Just *take me at my word* today, whatever that may mean.

I love you, my Beloved, and I always will. Fall in love with me.

Love,<br>Jesus

## Respond

Write a letter to Jesus, telling him all that is in your heart.

# Letter Twenty

## Listen

One was there who had been an invalid for thirty-eight years. When Jesus saw him lying there and learned that he had been in this condition for a long time, he asked him, "Do you want to get well?"

"Sir," the invalid replied, "I have no one to help me into the pool when the water is stirred. While I am trying to get in, someone else goes down ahead of me."

Then Jesus said to him, "Get up! Pick up you mat and walk." At once the man was cured; he picked up his mat and walked."
~John 5:5-8

## Reflect

My Beloved,

O how deeply I long for you to "get well." The only problem is that you have to want it too. You have to be willing to leave *life on the mat* behind.

I know you have somehow grown oddly comfortable in your brokenness and dysfunction. I know that you have gotten so used to *life on the mat* that you might not really want the responsibility that comes along with being healed and whole. That's why I asked you the question in the first place.

I see you lying there. I really see you. I don't just see your outward appearance, but I see all the way down into the depths of your being. I don't just see the brokenness of your body, I see the full brokenness of your soul. And, to be quite honest, your bodily brokenness is the least of your worries. But I can make you well. In fact, I long to make you well. Whenever my love and your brokenness collide, something beautiful is always born; there is healing and redemption and restoration.

But you need to know that if I do, indeed, make you well, you will have to "pick up your mat and walk." You cannot just return to life on the mat, as if nothing had happened. I love you too much to allow that. If I make you well, it will change everything, that's the way love works—it always transforms. Are you ready for that?

So, what will it be, Beloved? Do you want to get well?

Love,<br>Jesus

## Respond

Write a letter to Jesus, telling him all that is in your heart.

# Letter Twenty-One

## Listen

Jesus said to them, "My Father is always at his work to this very day, and I, too am working." ~John 5:17

## Reflect

My Beloved,

In this life, you will be tempted to believe that it is only during the good times that I am truly at work, but nothing could be further from the truth. I do not work only when things are going well; I am always at work, especially when times are hard. I do not just work in times of joy and gladness and abundance, but I also work when you are being disoriented, disturbed, and disrupted. I am at work in times of consolation and I am at work in times of desolation. In fact, the wisest of saints have learned to pay careful attention to the things that provoke and disrupt them, for those things are able to tell them a lot about where and how the Spirit is at work.

I am always trying, Beloved, to get your attention. I am always up to something very good within you, even when times don't appear so good. So pay attention to it all, because I am using all things to communicate my love to you. Allow all things—both good and bad—to help you fall more and more in love with me.

Love,<br>Jesus

## Respond

Write a letter to Jesus, telling him all that is in your heart.

# Letter Twenty-Two

# Listen

When Jesus looked up and saw a great crowd coming toward him, he said, "Where shall we buy bread for these people to eat?" He asked this only to test them, for he already had in mind what he was going to do.

Philip answered him, "Eight months wages would not buy enough bread for each one to have a bite!"

Another of his disciples, Andrew, Simon Peter's brother, spoke up, "Here is a boy with five small barley loaves and two small fish, but how far would they go among so many?"

Jesus said, "Have the people sit down." There was plenty of grass in that place, and the men sat down, about five thousand of them. Jesus then took the loaves, gave thanks, and distributed to those who were seated as much as they wanted. He did the same with the fish.

When they had all had enough to eat, he said to his disciples, "Gather the pieces that are left over. Let nothing be wasted." So they gathered them and filled twelve baskets with the pieces of the five barley loaves left over by those who had eaten. ~John 6:5-13

# Reflect

My Beloved,

I know that you live in constant fear that you are not enough. I know that most days you feel like you don't measure up; like you don't have what it takes to be the person or the spouse or the parent or the friend or the minister I have called you to be. I know that you don't feel like you have the resources available to meet all the needs and demands of the multitudes of hurting and hungry people coming your direction on a daily basis. And the truth is, you don't. But, luckily, I do. You don't have to be enough, because I am enough.

Just bring me what you've got, however meager it may seem. I will take it, break it, and then multiply it into something good and beautiful and abundant. And at the end of the day, when it is finally time to gather the broken pieces, there will even be *enough* left over for you. That's how much I love you, so fall in love with me.

Love,<br>Jesus

## Respond

Write a letter to Jesus, telling him all that is in your heart.

# Letter Twenty-Three

## Listen

When evening came, his disciples went down to the lake, where they got into a boat and set off across the lake for Capernaum. By now it was dark, and Jesus had not yet joined them. A strong wind was blowing and the water grew rough. When they had rowed three or three and a half miles, they saw Jesus approaching the boat, walking on the water; and they were terrified. But he said to them, "It is I: don't be afraid." Then they we willing to take him into the boat, and immediately the boat reached the shore where they were heading. ~John 6:16-21

## Reflect

My Beloved,

There are going to be storms in this life, that much is certain. And many of these storms will be of the overwhelming variety. Some you will see coming from a long way off, and some with take you completely by surprise. Just remember that when the skies grow dark and the waters get rough and you wonder if you are going to be able to survive the wind and the waves, do not be afraid, for I am with you. I have not left you to manage these storms alone. Just look for me; I am there. I will come out to you, walking on the sea. I will meet you in the midst of the chaos and will keep you from perishing. All you have to do is trust me.

Love,<br>
Jesus

## Respond

Write a letter to Jesus, telling him all that is in your heart.

# Letter Twenty-Four

# Listen

Then Jesus declared, "I am the bread of life. He who comes to me will never go hungry, and he who believes in me will never be thirsty. But as I told you, you have seen me and still you do not believe." ~John 6:35-36

# Reflect

My Beloved,

One of the main strategies of the enemy is to get you to feed on anything other than me, the Bread of Life. He will come to you when you are at your weakest and most vulnerable point, and he will fill your head with all sorts of lies and deception. He will encourage you to meet legitimate needs in illegitimate ways. He will use your desires for love and impact against you, trying to convince you that these legitimate needs can only be met by earthly means. Thus, he will lure you away from me with all kinds of quick solutions and cheap substitutes. But don't fall for his tricks, they are hollow and lifeless. They have no substance.

There is only one *bread* that can truly satisfy, and that is me, the Bread of Life. There is only one source of love and impact that can satisfy the deepest desires of your heart and soul, everything else is just cotton candy; the more you eat, the less it satisfies. You see, the things of this world may taste good to the mouth, but they cannot offer any real satisfaction to the deepest longings of your soul.

So don't fall into the trap of feeding on the things of this world, when only the things of God can truly satisfy. Do not feed on success, or affirmation, or achievement. Don't be seduced away from me by the wiles of money, power, and popularity. Don't demand that those in your life and world meet needs that they were never intended to fully meet. That is far too much pressure to put on anyone. Instead, let me meet those needs so that you can love them, rather than constantly trying to extort love out of them. Feed on me, my Beloved. Let my love fill you. Then, fall in love with me.

Love,<br>
Jesus

## Respond

Write a letter to Jesus, telling him all that is in your heart.

# Letter Twenty-Five

## Listen

Jesus said to them, "I tell you the truth, unless you eat the flesh of the Son of Man and drink his blood, you have no life in you. Whoever eats my flesh and drinks my blood has eternal life, and I will raise him up on the last day. For my flesh is real food and my blood is real drink. Whoever eats my flesh and drinks my blood remains in me, and I in him. Just as the living Father sent me and I live because of the Father, so the one who feeds on me will live because of me. This is the bread that came down from heaven. Your forefathers ate manna and died, but he who feeds on this bread will live forever." ~John 6:53-58

## Reflect

My Beloved,

It is my blood
that gives you life,
it is my blood
that flows with love,
it is my blood
that makes you whole.

It is my blood
I want coursing
through your veins,
it is my blood
I want animating
your existence.

I offer you my body
and my blood,
so that my life
and my love

might be in you
and might run
through you.

So eat and drink
my Beloved,
feed on me.
For unless you do,
you will have
no life in you.

Love,
Jesus

## Respond

Write a poem to Jesus, telling him all that is in your heart.

# Letter Twenty-Six

# Listen

On the last and greatest day of the Feast, Jesus stood and said in a loud voice, "If anyone is thirsty, let him come to me and drink. Whoever believes in me, as the Scripture has said, streams of living water will flow from within him." ~John 7:37-38

# Reflect

My Beloved,

I made you for fullness and abundance, not for emptiness and scarcity. But, unfortunately, you do not often experience the fullness I made you for, so you try to manufacture it yourself.

That's what the Father was talking about when he said through the prophet Jeremiah: "My people have committed two sins: They have forsaken me, the spring of living water, and have dug their own cisterns, broken cisterns that cannot hold water." (Jer. 2:13) I alone am the spring of living water. The very best you can hope for apart from me is partial or temporary fullness—a broken cistern that cannot hold water. You may feel full for a while, but eventually all of that fullness will leak right out.

I am the only one who can fill you, my Beloved. Do you really believe that? Do you believe that I am the spring of living water? Do you really believe that I want fullness and abundance for you? And do you really believe that I am the only one who can give it to you?

This very day, I say to you, "If anyone is thirsty, let him come to me and drink. Whoever believes in me, as the Scripture has said, streams of living water will flow from within him." I love you, my Beloved, and want you to experience the life and the fullness and the abundance I created you for. Fall in love with me so you can do just that.

Love,<br>Jesus

## Respond

Write a letter to Jesus, telling him all that is in your heart.

# Letter Twenty-Seven

## Listen

At dawn he appeared again in the temple courts, where all the people gathered around him, and he sat down to teach them. The teachers of the law and the Pharisees brought in a woman caught in adultery. They made her stand before the group and said to Jesus, "Teacher, this woman was caught in the act of adultery. In the Law Moses commanded us to stone such women. Now what do you say?" They were using this question as a trap, in order to have a basis for accusing him.

But Jesus bent down and started to write on the ground with his finger. When they kept on questioning him, he straightened up and said to them, "If any one of you is without sin, let him be the first to throw a stone at her." Again he stooped down and wrote on the ground.

At this, those who heard began to go away one at a time, the older ones first, until only Jesus was left, with the woman still standing there. Jesus straightened up and asked her, "Woman, where are they? Has no one condemned you?"

"No one, sir," she said.

"Then neither do I condemn you," Jesus declared. "Go and leave your life of sin." ~John 8:2-11

## Reflect

O My Dearest Children,

Why do you treat one another this way? Why are you so quick to want to throw stones at each other? Why do you take such delight in attacks and insults and condemnations? Why such venom, such poison constantly spewing from your lips? Why do you revel in each other's inadequacies, misfortunes, and failures? Do you really feel that horrible about yourselves, and about your own lack of value and worth, that you find some kind of misguided pleasure in tearing others down, so that you might be built up?

O My Dear Children, this is not my way! My way is love, not condemnation. I do not throw stones, I forgive. I do not attack, I serve. I do not react, I listen. I do not condemn you, therefore do not condemn one another. Put down your stones, pick up my love, and take it to the world. It is the natural result of falling more and more in love with me.

Love,<br>Jesus

## Respond

Write a letter to Jesus, telling him all that is in your heart.

# Letter Twenty-Eight

## Listen

So Jesus said to the Jews who had believed him, "If you abide in my word, you are truly my disciples, and you will know the truth, and the truth will set you free." ~John 8:31-32

## Reflect

My Beloved,

It is only the truth that can set you free, and you can only know that truth by abiding in my word. Not just by reading it, not just by studying it, not just by memorizing it, but by abiding in it. Make your home in my word, and let my word make its home in you. Let it bring you to life inside and breathe its divine breath within you. If you do that, then you will be well on your way to the life of freedom I most deeply want for you. You will not be easily led astray by the many lies that the world and the culture and your fallen flesh want you to believe. For believing the lies always leads to bondage, but believing the truth always leads to freedom.

Let my word be what forms and shapes and molds you. Let it be what determines who you are and what you do. If you abide in my word, you will know the truth, and the truth will set you free.

Love,<br>
Jesus

## Respond

Write a letter to Jesus, telling him all that is in your heart.

# Letter Twenty-Nine

# Listen

Jesus heard that they had thrown him out, and when he found him, he said, "Do you believe in the Son of Man?"

"Who is he, sir?" the man asked. "Tell me so that I may believe in him."

Jesus said, "You have now seen him; in fact, he is the one speaking with you."

Then the man said, "Lord, I believe," and he worshipped him.

Jesus said, "For judgment I have come into this world, so that the blind will see and those who see will become blind."

Some Pharisees who were with him heard him say this and asked, "What? Are we blind too?"

Jesus said, "If you were blind, you would not be guilty of sin; but now that you claim to see, your guilt remains." ~John 9:35-41

# Reflect

My Beloved,

Nothing warms my heart quite like making a blind man see. There is just something so magical about that moment in time when everything is unveiled, afresh and anew; when someone who has never known color or vibrancy or depth or contrast or beauty is suddenly seized by all of them at once. It is a moment of sheer wonder and delight.

On the other hand, nothing saddens my heart more than someone who claims they can see, when they are really blind. They already think they know everything, so there is no need to really look. There is no need to pay attention, because their sense of holy curiosity has died long ago. There is no longer any room within them for discovery, no spirit of wonder, no attitude of awe and amazement. The mystery has been taken out of life because they "see" things so clearly, but they really don't see at all.

So, my Beloved, always keep your sense of wonder about you. Always be willing to see with fresh eyes and be willing to hear with fresh ears. Always be ready to embrace the mystery and the uniqueness of the life that is happening around and within you. It will make you fall more and more in love with me each day.

Love,<br>Jesus

## Respond

Write a letter to Jesus, telling him all that is in your heart.

# Letter Thirty

## Listen

"The thief comes only to steal and kill and destroy; I have come that they may have life, and have it to the full." ~John 10:10

## Reflect

My Beloved,

Be careful. You have an adversary. He is a liar and a thief. He cannot be trusted. His only desire is to steal, kill, and destroy. He will try to convince you that you are unlovable, that there is no hope for you, and that you can never change. If that doesn't work, he will try to convince you that you are doing just fine and have no need of me. He will even try to convince you that the fullness and life that I offer is somehow inferior to that of the world. He does this because he wants you to feast on less-wild lovers, rather than on me, the Lover of your Soul. So be careful, his tricks are many. He is out to rob you of true life by getting you to engage in cheap imitations of it. He is out to keep you from your truest self by making you believe that the false self is all there is. Ultimately, he is trying to get you to settle for less, because less is all he has to offer. That is the brilliance of his deception; somehow he is able to make less look like more.

Just know that I am the good shepherd, my Beloved. I am the one who truly loves you. I am the only one who can give you the fullness and life you were made for. Come to me and you will live. Fall in love with me, and you will know true life and true love.

Love,
Jesus

# Respond

Write a letter to Jesus, telling him all that is in your heart.

# Letter Thirty-One

# Listen

"I am the good shepherd; I know my sheep and my sheep know me—just as the Father knows me and I know the Father—and I lay down my life for the sheep." ~John 10:14-15

# Reflect

My Beloved,

I am the good shepherd; I know every single thing about you. I know your hopes and your dreams, I know your wants and your needs, I know your fears and your insecurities, and I even know your patterns and your dysfunctions. I know your greatest joys and I know your deepest sorrows. I know your strengths and I know your weaknesses. I know your strongholds and I know your vulnerabilities. No one knows you like I do, my Little Lamb. And because no one knows you like I do, no one can take care of you like I can. I would do anything for you, even lay down my life. There is nothing you will ever need that I cannot provide. I love you so much, my Little Lamb; fall in love with me.

Love,
Jesus

# Respond

Write a letter to Jesus, telling him all that is in your heart.

# Letter Thirty-Two

# Listen

Now a man named Lazarus was sick. He was from Bethany; the village of Mary and her sister Martha. This Mary, whose brother Lazarus now lay sick, was the same one who poured perfume on the Lord and wiped his feet with her hair. So the sisters sent word to Jesus, "Lord, the one you love is sick."

When he heard this, Jesus said, "This sickness will not end in death. No, it is for God's glory so that God's Son may be glorified through it." Jesus loved Martha and her sister and Lazarus. Yet when he heard that Lazarus was sick, he stayed where he was for two more days. ~John 11:1-6

# Reflect

My Beloved,

Sometimes my love will not make sense to you. Sometimes it may seem like I've left you hanging out to dry. That's because you do not see what I see and you do not know what I know. Thus, there are times in this life when you are just going to have to trust me.

The truth is that some of the things in this life that look like they could only be terrible, hold some of life's richest gifts, blessings, and possibilities. They are the stuff of extraordinary growth, and are some of the best opportunities for me to show up in a way that leaves everyone saying, "Wow!"

And some of the things in this life that look for all the world like they would be good and wonderful things, simply aren't. They are empty and hollow and meaningless—easy and comfortable are seldom best. So sometimes, for no apparent reason, it's just best for me *to stay put for a couple of days*, even when it appears like it's not the most loving thing to do.

The bottom line, my Beloved, is that during these times you are going to have to learn to trust my heart, even when you can't see my hand. I desire the best for you and am constantly working for your good. Trust in my love.

Love,<br>Jesus

## Respond

Write a letter to Jesus, telling him all that is in your heart.

# Letter Thirty-Three

## Listen

When he had said this, Jesus called out in a loud voice, "Lazarus, come out!" The dead man came out, his hands and feet wrapped with strips of linen, and a cloth was around his face.

Jesus said to them, "Take off the grave clothes and let him go."
~John 11:43-44

## Reflect

My Beloved,

Come out! Leave behind the cold, dark tomb, take off the grave clothes that bind and hinder you, and come out into the light of new life. It is the life you were created for — resurrection life.

Never again settle for death, decay, and decomposition, when you can have life and joy and freedom. Allow my voice to raise you up and make you new. I am the resurrection and the life, whoever believes in me will live even though he dies. Your death will merely be the gateway to new life, for I am the God who is forever calling my loved ones out of the tomb.

So come out, my Beloved, come out of that tomb, take off those grave clothes, and enter into the resurrection life I'm calling you to.

                                              Love,
                                              Jesus

## Respond

Write a letter to Jesus, telling him all that is in your heart.

# Letter Thirty-Four

## Listen

Here a dinner was given in Jesus' honor, Martha served, while Lazarus was among those reclining at the table with him. Then Mary took about a pint of pure nard, an expensive perfume; she poured it on Jesus' feet and wiped his feet with her hair. And the house was filled with the fragrance of the perfume. ~John 12:2-3

## Reflect

My Beloved,

More than anything I want your affection. O how I long for an extravagant gesture of uninhibited love. Duty and obligation can only get you so far. At some point, your heart has to be so full of love for me that it simply cannot contain itself, it must be poured out. That's how life was designed to be; affection always precedes genuine transformation. For it is an unbridled affection for me that determines the order of all your other affections.

So how will you show me your love today, Beloved? How will you pour it out? What will you do in response to being seized by the power of my great affection?

It's all about love, Beloved, so fall in love with me.

Love,<br>Jesus

## Respond

Write a letter to Jesus, telling him all that is in your heart.

# Letter Thirty-Five

## Listen

Jesus replied, "The hour has come for the Son of Man to be glorified. I tell you the truth, unless a kernel of wheat falls to the ground and dies, it remains only a single seed. But if it dies, it produces many seeds. The man who loves his life will lose it, while the man who hates his life in this world will keep it for eternal life." ~John 12:23-25

## Reflect

My Beloved,

Make no mistake about it, in the Kingdom of God you save your life by losing it. Unless a kernel of wheat falls to the ground and dies, it remains only a single seed. But if it dies, it produces many seeds. That's how life works in my kingdom: death always precedes new life. Unless you first let go of your old ways of being and seeing, new ways will never have the space and time to emerge and grow. Until you first are willing to let go of your old habits and patterns and dysfunctions, new ones can never be established. Unless you die to sin, you will never really be able to live unto God.

It is the Paschal mystery: nothing that has not died will ever be resurrected. You must be crucified with me, so that you no longer live, but I live in you. (Gal. 2:20) Which means that life is no longer about living according to your own preferences, but according to mine. It means that life is no longer about your own purpose and direction, but about mine. It means that life is no longer about your own dreams and desires, but about my dreams and desires for you. It means that life is no longer about you, but about me.

So I ask you this, Beloved, what must die in you during this season, in order for something beautiful to be born? Because that's what life with me is really all about. .

Love,<br>Jesus

## Respond

Write a letter to Jesus, telling him all that is in your heart.

# Letter Thirty-Six

## Listen

It was just before the Passover Feast. Jesus knew that the time had come for him to leave this world and go to the Father. Having loved his own who were in the world, he now showed them the full extent of his love.

The evening meal was being served, and the devil had already prompted Judas Iscariot, son of Simon, to betray Jesus. Jesus knew that the Father had put all things under his power, and that he had come from God and was returning to God; so he got up from the meal, took off his outer clothing, and wrapped a towel around his waist. After that, he poured water into a basin and began to wash the disciples' feet, drying them with the towel that was around his waist. ~John 13:1-5

## Reflect

My Beloved,

Tonight I kneel before you, a towel wrapped around my waist. I look deeply into your eyes and gently take your dirty feet into my strong and tender hands. They must be washed. So I pour water into a basin and I begin to wash your feet.

I do this to show you the full extent of my extravagant love. I do this to show you your immense value and worth. I do this as an example, so that you can do as I have done for you. So go, my Beloved, go and stoop down. Take the lowest place. Wash the dirtiest feet. Show people how fully and deeply they are loved. By this all men will know that you are my disciples.

Love,<br>
Jesus

# Respond

Write a letter to Jesus, telling him all that is in your heart.

# Letter Thirty-Seven

## Listen

Simon Peter asked him, "Lord, where are you going?"

Jesus replied, "Where I am going, you cannot follow now, but you will follow later."

Peter asked, "Lord, why can't I follow now? I will lay down my life for you?"

Then Jesus answered, "Will you really lay down your life for me? I tell you the truth, before the rooster crows, you will disown me three times!" ~John 13:36-38

## Reflect

My Beloved,

Will you really lay down your life for me? Will you really lay aside all privilege and power and preference, and put me before all else? Will you really place yourself wholly and unreservedly in my hands? Will you really deny yourself and take up your cross and follow me, even to places you would rather not go? Will you really empty yourself of self, so that you may be full of me? Will you really become nothing, so that I might become everything? Will you really surrender all that you are and all that you have to my rule and my care? Will you really? Or, before the morning comes, will you have denied that you even know me?

I love you, my Beloved, no matter what. Never forget that, and fall more in love with me as a result.

Love,<br>
Jesus

# Respond

Write a letter to Jesus, telling him all that is in your heart.

# Letter Thirty-Eight

## Listen

Let not your hearts be troubled. Trust in God; trust also in me. In my Father's house are many rooms, if it were not so, I would have told you. I am going there to prepare a place for you. And if I go and prepare a place for you, I will come back and take you to be with me that you may also be where I am. ~John 14:1-2

## Reflect

My Beloved,

The day we were betrothed to one another, my beautiful bride, I spoke these very words of promise and of love and of hope to you. That very day, I set out for my Father's house, to build a place in which we could live in union and harmony and bliss, forever and ever. And I promised you that if I went to prepare that place, I would return and take you back to be with me, so that you would be where I am. You and I living in intimate, loving, eternal union.

Today, that promise still holds true, my Love. So do not let your heart be troubled. Do not allow the cares and concerns and hardships of this life to cause you to lose hope in our love. Trust in God, Beloved; trust also in me. I will come again and take you home to be with me forever. Hang in there, for I am coming soon.

Love,<br>
Jesus

## Respond

Write a letter to Jesus, telling him all that is in your heart.

# Letter Thirty-Nine

## Listen

Jesus replied, "If anyone loves me, he will obey my teaching. My Father will love him, and we will come and make our home with him." ~John 14:23

## Reflect

My Beloved,

You were created with a longing for home buried deep within you. You know what I'm talking about, don't you? It's that feeling of being right where you're supposed to be, and being with the people you were made to be with. It is that place of true belonging and total acceptance. It is that place where you are loved and cared for in a way that is unlike any other. There's just something so right about it.

Home is meant to be a place of wholeness and rest and peace, a place of safety and of true shalom, a place where everything is as it's supposed to be. Home is meant to be a place where we are able to experience the creation intent of God.

Home is the place I made you for. That's why the longing for home is so deeply woven into the fabric of your being. I put it there and I am the only one who can totally satisfy it. It is the place where you are most alive, most at peace, most free, most loved, and most yourself.

Make your home in me, my Beloved, and I will make my home in you.

Love,<br>
Jesus

# Respond

Write a letter to Jesus, telling him all that is in your heart.

# Letter Forty

# Listen

"Abide in me, and I will abide in you. As the branch cannot bear fruit by itself, unless it abides in the vine, neither can you, unless you abide in me. I am the vine; you are the branches. Whoever abides in me and I in him, he it is that bears much fruit, for apart from me you can do nothing." ~John 15:4-5

# Reflect

My Beloved,

There are few things in this life that are more important than abiding—you in me and me in you. In fact, abiding is the key to the entire spiritual journey. To abide (*menō*) means to remain, to stay, or to dwell in. When you abide in me, you remain intimately connected to me, the way a branch is connected to a vine. I become your one true source of life and health and fruit. And your soul becomes a beautiful branch, teeming with love, joy, peace, patience, kindness, goodness, faithfulness, gentleness, and self-control.

Unfortunately, abiding doesn't just happen on its own; it doesn't just fall on your head. It takes some practice. It requires both attention and intention. If you are not intentional about abiding in me, you will abide in someone or something else. You will abide in your fears, your worries, and your doubts. Or you will abide in your insecurities, your wounds, and your dysfunctions. Or you will abide in your ambitions, your successes, and your achievements. The list is endless. Suffice it to say that only when you abide in me will your life produce the kind of joy and delight you were created to produce; for *apart from me, you can do nothing*.

So abide in me, my Beloved, and I will abide in you. Stay connected to me, your source of life and joy and love. It will make you into who and what you were intended to be.

Love,<br>Jesus

## Respond

Write a letter to Jesus, telling him all that is in your heart.

# Letter Forty-One

## Listen

"I tell you the truth, you will weep and mourn while the world rejoices. You will grieve, but your grief will turn to joy. A woman giving birth to a child has pain because her time has come; but when her baby is born she forgets the anguish because of her joy that a child is born into the world. So with you: Now is your time of grief, but I will see you again and you will rejoice, and no one will take away your joy." ~John 16:20-22

## Reflect

My Beloved,

There will be a lot of weeping and mourning in this life. There will be times of great sorrow and sadness and pain; you will grieve losses and groan inequities and mourn monstrosities. And for a while it will appear that evil and chaos and calamity reign free. But it is only for a time; I will return and make all things right again. In the end, I will redeem your pain and loss and grief and sorrow and sadness, and turn it into joy.

So, in the meantime, wait in hope. Trust in my unfailing love and care. "For with the Lord is unfailing love and with him is full redemption. He himself will redeem Israel from all their sins," (Psalm 130:7-8) and sorrow and sadness and pain. So fear not, though darkness may abound for a while, there will be joy in the morning.

Love,<br>
Jesus

# Respond

Write a letter to Jesus, telling him all that is in your heart.

# Letter Forty-Two

## Listen

"A time is coming, and has come, when you will be scattered, each to his own home. You will leave me all alone. Yet I am not alone, for my Father is with me."

"I have told you these things, so that in me you may have peace. In this world you will have trouble. But take heart! I have overcome the world." ~John 16:31-33

## Reflect

My Beloved,

Always remember that my faithfulness to you is not dependent upon your faithfulness to me. There will be times in your life when you will scatter, times when you will fall, times when you will fail. But rest assured, my relationship with you doesn't depend on your grip on me, but on my grip on you. I will hold you, I will keep you, and I will sustain you. In fact, somehow in the strange economy of God, your failures will actually help you to better know and enjoy the depths of my love.

Don't get me wrong, I am not giving you license to fall or fail, I am just telling you the truth. You will fall, you will fail, but these fallings and failings are not final. My love and my faithfulness are final. So take heart! I have overcome the world.

Love,<br>Jesus

## Respond

Write a letter to Jesus, telling him all that is in your heart.

# Letter Forty-Three

# Listen

"I pray also for those who will believe in me through their message, that all of them may be one, Father, just as you are in me and I am in you. May they also be in us so that the world may believe that you have sent me. I have given them the glory that you gave me, that they may be one as we are one. I in them and you in me. May they be brought to complete unity to let the world know that you sent me and have loved them even as you have loved me." ~John 17:20-23

# Reflect

My Dear Children,

In the upper room, the night before my suffering and death, I prayed for you. I prayed that all of you would be one, as the Father and I are one. Why did I pray for that? Because oneness is a beautiful reflection to the world of the goodness and love and delight of the One who made you. It is a oneness that is winsome and attractive; drawing people toward it like moths to a flame. That's because it is a oneness that every created thing was made from, and a oneness that every created thing was made for. Thus, when the world tastes this oneness, it tastes the goodness of its Creator; the goodness spoken of in Genesis 1:31. In other words, it tastes the creation intent of God. This oneness will resonate so deeply with their spirits that it will remind them of a goodness they desperately long for, but have long since forgotten. It will actually begin to roll back the effects of the Fall.

So, my dear children, work hard at maintaining this oneness; it is a vital part of revealing my love and my character to this lost and broken world. And nothing breaks my heart more than division, disunity, and dissension. So work hard not to be petty or contentious or critical, they do not reflect my heart and should not be a part of my people.

Instead, love one another well, serve one another sacrificially, and go out of your way to honor and respect one another. Do the hard work of reconciliation when it is necessary. Live in harmony and joy and peace, for when you live in unity with one another you show the world how it was really supposed to be. You show them how good I really am. The life I want for you, my children, is meant to reflect the Divine Life, so be one as the Father and I are one.

Love,<br>Jesus

## Respond

Write a letter to Jesus, telling him all that is in your heart.

# Letter Forty-Four

# Listen

Jesus, knowing all that was going to happen to him, went out and asked them, "Who is it you want?"

"Jesus of Nazareth," they replied.

"I am he," Jesus said. (And Judas the traitor was standing there with them.) When he said, "I am he," they drew back and fell to the ground.

Again he asked the, "Who is it you want?"

And they said, "Jesus of Nazareth."

"I told you that I am he," Jesus answered. "If you are looking for me, then let these men go." This happened so that the words he had spoken would be fulfilled: "I have not lost one of those you gave me."

Then Simon Peter, who had a sword, drew it and struck the high priest's servant, cutting off his right ear. (The servant's name was Malchus.)

Jesus commanded Peter, "Put your sword away! Shall I not drink the cup the Father has given me?" ~John 18:4-11

# Reflect

My Beloved,

My suffering and death was not a surprise to me. I knew all along, since before eternity, everything that would happen, and I said "yes" to all of it because of my great love for my Father and my unfailing love for you. No one was taking me against my will, I was volunteering to die, so that you might live. I would rather die for you than live without you. That's the love story the Father and I were writing.

The cross was not a backup plan; the cross was always *the* plan. It was meant to show you the full extent of my love. It was the "cup" I signed up for. It was the cup I chose to drink because of my love for you. Shall I not drink the cup the Father has given me?

And shall you not drink it as well? Will you, my Beloved, live your life like I did? Will you live a life of love and self-sacrifice? Will you lay down your life for others, instead of drawing your sword and cutting off their ears?

I laid down my life for you, Beloved, because I love you. Now, fall in love with me and lay down your lives for one another.

Love,<br>
Jesus

## Respond

Write a letter to Jesus, telling him all that is in your heart.

# Letter Forty-Five

# Listen

Then the detachment of soldiers with its commander and the Jewish officials arrested Jesus. They bound him and brought him first to Annas, who was the father-in-law of Caiaphas, the high priest that year. ~John 18:12-13

# Reflect

My Beloved,

Mere ropes could not bind the hands of the King of kings and Lord of lords; the hands that held the waters of the earth in its hollow and marked off the heavens with its span. (Isaiah 40:12) The hands that gave sight to the blind, healed the sick, and raised the dead. The hands that multiplied the loaves and the fishes to feed the multitudes. Could mere ropes hold those hands? Of course not, only love could do that. I allowed my hands to be bound because of my passionate, extravagant, sacrificial love for you.

There was no pain too great to endure for you. There was no depth too low to descend. There was no humiliation too extreme to embrace, in order to show you the depths of my love.

Now, I want you to go and love like that as well. How else will the world know what I have done for them?

I love you, my Beloved. Fall in love with me.

Love,<br>Jesus

# Respond

Write a letter to Jesus, telling him all that is in your heart.

# Letter Forty-Six

# Listen

As Simon Peter stood warming himself, he was asked, "You are not one of his disciples are you?"

He denied it, saying, "I am not."

One of the high priest's servants, a relative of the man whose ear Peter had cut off, challenged him, "Didn't I see you with him in the olive grove?" Again Peter denied it, and at that moment a rooster began to crow. ~John 18:25-27

# Reflect

My Beloved,

There will be times in your walk with me when you'll think you've done something so awful that it cannot possibly be forgiven; something that is beyond the reach of my grace. You will fall and you will fail. You will disappoint and you will disobey. You will deny and you will abandon. But fear not, these moments are not final. They do not define you. Nothing can separate you from my love. In fact, as crazy as it may sound, I will actually use those events and experiences to help you love me more. Somehow I will use them, as I did with Simon Peter, to help you better understand the depths of my grace and my forgiveness, so that you may better offer them to this broken and hurting world.

Don't get me wrong, I'm not giving you permission to do those things, but I am letting you know that they need not define you. So don't be defined by your failures and mistakes, but be defined by my love. Allow my love and my grace and my forgiveness to capture your heart and seize your affections. If you do that, you will have no choice but to become the person I made you to be. It is the nature of my love to transform everyone and everything it comes in contact with. My desire is that you know the heights and depths and breadth of my love, and allow that love to make you fall more and more in love with me.

Love,<br>Jesus

## Respond

Write a letter to Jesus, telling him all that is in your heart.

# Letter Forty-Seven

## Listen

Then Pilate took Jesus and had him flogged. The soldiers twisted together a crown of thorns and put it on his head. They clothed him in a purple robe and went up to him again and again, saying, "Hail, king of the Jews!" And they struck him in the face. ~John 19:1-3

## Reflect

My Beloved,

Wounds. This life is so full of wounds. And you, my dear one, have been deeply wounded in so many ways. So many people and experiences and events have left their mark on you, and it simply breaks my heart. That was not the way this life was intended to be. I made you out of love, for joy and peace and wholeness. And yet, here you are, bruised and battered and beaten.

That's why I came. I came to redeem your wounds. I came to take them on myself, because I was wounded too. I know what it's like to be beaten and bludgeoned and abused. I know what it's like to be lonely and betrayed and abandoned. I know what it's like to be the object of hatred and anger and scorn. I know what it's like to be called names and to be mocked and to be made fun of. I know what it is like to be discriminated against and oppressed and treated unjustly. I know it all. There is nothing that you will experience in this life that I cannot understand, because not only was I wounded in my life on earth, but I also took all of your wounds upon myself, so that you might be healed and made whole again.

"I was despised and rejected by men, a man of sorrows, and familiar with suffering. Like one from whom men hide their faces. I was despised, and the world esteemed me not. But surely I took up your infirmities and carried your sorrows. I was considered stricken by God, smitten by him, and afflicted. I was pierced for your transgressions, I was crushed for your iniquities, and the punishment that brought you peace was upon me. In fact, it is by my wounds that you are healed." (Is. 53:3-5) I became wounded, so that you might be healed and made whole.

That's how much I love you, my Beloved. Fall in love with me.

Love,<br>Jesus

## Respond

Write a letter to Jesus, telling him all that is in your heart.

# Letter Forty-Eight

## Listen

Finally Pilate handed him over to be crucified. So the soldiers took charge of Jesus. Carrying his own cross, he went out to the place of the Skull (which in Aramaic is called Golgotha). Here they crucified him, and with him two others — one on each side and Jesus in the middle. ~John 19:16-18

## Reflect

O My Beloved,

If you ever begin to doubt my love, if you ever begin to question your own value and worth, if you ever begin to wonder what I really think about you, just look at the cross and let it remove all doubt. Look deeply into my eyes, the eyes of the Crucified One, as I hang upon that tree, and see the love they hold for you. I want you to be totally and completely convinced that you are fully and deeply and passionately and unconditionally loved.

That is how much I love you, my Beloved, so fall in love with me.

Love,<br>Jesus

## Respond

Write a letter to Jesus, telling him all that is in your heart.

# Letter Forty-Nine

## Listen

Later, knowing that all was now completed, and so that the Scripture would be fulfilled, Jesus said, "I am thirsty." A jar of wine vinegar was there, so they soaked a sponge on a stalk of the hyssop plant, and lifted it to Jesus' lips. When he had received the drink, Jesus said, "It is finished." With that, he bowed his head and gave up his spirit. ~John 19:28-30

## Reflect

My Beloved,

It is finished! It really is finished! Nothing else needs to be added to what was done at the cross. It is completely and totally sufficient for you. It does not depend on your own efforts, your own achievements, your own accomplishments, or even your own righteousness. You do not have to try and justify your own existence anymore, it has been done for you. You are fully and freely justified by my work on the cross. It is finished. Live in the truth and the freedom of that reality. Let your life be a joyful and loving response to what has already been done for you.

Live in the fullness and freedom of my love, my Beloved, and fall more and more in love with me.

Love,<br>Jesus

## Respond

Write a letter to Jesus, telling him all that is in your heart.

# Letter Fifty

## Listen

At the place where Jesus was crucified, there was a garden, and in the garden a new tomb, in which no one had ever been laid. Because it was the Jewish day of Preparation and since the tomb was nearby, they laid Jesus there. ~John 19:41-42

## Reflect

My Beloved,

Do not be afraid of the tomb, it is a necessary part of this life; no one can avoid it. Do not fear death, because, in my kingdom, death is not final; it is merely the gateway to new life. In the words of a wise saint, "Nothing that has not died will be resurrected."

So, my Beloved, always remember that, "To live is Christ and to die is gain." (Phil. 1:21) Did you get that? To die is gain! Notice, it doesn't say, "To live is gain and to die is Christ." Yet so many—even some of my very own—seem to live that way. But not you, Beloved. See death for what it really is, a beautiful beginning instead of a tragic ending.

And since death always makes room for new life, my dear one, I ask you today, what needs to die in you, in order to make room for something new to be born? For the final death is not the only one that matters. In the spiritual life, there are thousands of smaller deaths before that.

I love you so much, My Beloved, and I long for you to know and experience life, so fall in love with me and you will.

Love,<br>Jesus

# Respond

Write a letter to Jesus, telling him all that is in your heart.

# Letter Fifty-One

# Listen

Early on the first day of the week, while it was still dark, Mary Magdalene went to the tomb and saw that the stone had been rolled away from the entrance. ~John 20:1-2

# Reflect

My Beloved,

Between death and new life, between darkness and the morning light, there always exists a stone that must be rolled away. It is a stone that is much too heavy for you to move on your own, but fear not, nothing is too big for me. In fact, I specialize in rolling stones away. And the bigger, the better.

What stones exist in your life, Beloved? What stones keep you trapped in the death and darkness and hopelessness and gloom of the tomb? What stones have you tried and tried and tried to roll away, but they are just too big for you to budge?

I can roll those stones away. In fact, I would love to roll those stones away; all you have to do is ask. All you have to do is truly desire the life that lies on the other side of the tomb more than you desire to live in the deadness and darkness and stench of death.

I want life for you, Beloved, not death, so choose life. Choose my love, and fall more and more in love with me as a result.

Love,<br>
Jesus

# Respond

Write a letter to Jesus, telling him all that is in your heart.

# Letter Fifty-Two

# Listen

Mary stood outside the empty tomb crying. As she wept, she bent over to look into the tomb and saw two angels in white, seated where Jesus' body had been, one at the head and the other at the foot.

They asked her, "Woman, why are you crying?"

"They have taken my Lord away," she said, "and I don't know where they have put him." At this, she turned around and saw Jesus standing there, but she did not realize that it was Jesus.

"Woman," he said, "why are you crying? Who is it you are looking for?"

Thinking he was the gardener, she said, "Sir, if you have carried him away, tell me where you have put him, and I will get him."

Jesus said to her, "Mary."

She turned toward him and cried in Aramaic, "Rabboni!" (which means Teacher). ~John 20:11-16

# Reflect

My Beloved,

Why are you crying? Who is it you are looking for? What is the main source of the pain and sadness and disappointment and brokenness in your life these days? Where has death gotten the upper hand and made you doubt that you will ever see life again? Where are you dead inside and longing to experience resurrection? And who, or what, do you think can make you whole and free and alive again?

Come with Mary to the empty tomb, my Beloved. Bring all of your sorrow and sadness to me. Hear me as I call your name. Let my voice give you life and joy and hope. Let it raise up in you those parts that are dead and dying. I have conquered the grave, so that, through me, you can conquer it as well.

So go ahead and grieve the death in and around you, but never let it blind you to the life that is standing right in front of you. I am the Risen One and I love you so very much. Fall in love with me, my Beloved.

Love,<br>Jesus

## Respond

Write a letter to Jesus, telling him all that is in your heart.

# Letter Fifty-Three

# Listen

Jesus said, "Don't cling to me for I have not yet returned to the Father." ~John 20:17

# Reflect

My Beloved,

Never forget that I am too big for you. I'm too much for you to handle. I'm more than you can ever fully know or comprehend. You can never quite get your arms around me; you can never get to the end of me. So, in some ways, you are going to have to hold me very loosely, because the *me* you currently know is such a small part of who I really am.

This life is about constantly letting go of the *me* you think you know, in order to experience me in my fullness. This will be a lifelong process, not because I am ever-changing, for I am not, but because you are. As you grow and learn, you will find that I get bigger, not smaller. The more you know of me, the more you discover what there is to know. It's like peeling the layers of an onion, except the further in you go, the bigger I get, and the bigger my love for you becomes. So fall in love with me, my Beloved, as you come to know me more deeply.

Love,
Jesus

# Respond

Write a letter to Jesus, telling him all that is in your heart.

# Letter Fifty-Four

## Listen

On the evening of the first day of the week, when the disciples were together, with the doors locked for fear of the Jews, Jesus came and stood among them and said, "Peace be with you!" After he said this, he showed them his hands and side. The disciples were overjoyed when they saw the Lord. ~John 20:19-20

## Reflect

My Beloved,

Look at my hands and my side. See my wounds, which now are risen. Risen wounds are meant to be a source of life and healing and hope to all who see and encounter them.

Your wounds can become the same. In fact, your wounds were intended to become the same, once they are risen. Once they are resurrected and healed and redeemed, your risen wounds can be the absolute best thing about you. They can offer hope and healing and wholeness (*shalom*) to all who touch them. That is the way I designed ministry to be. So don't lead with your strengths, but lead with your risen wounds, the same way I did. That is the power of the gospel. That is how lives are changed. I know it sounds crazy, but *my power is made perfect in weakness.* (2 Cor. 12:9) So be weak, so that I can be strong in and through you.

Love,
Jesus

## Respond

Write a letter to Jesus, telling him all that is in your heart.

# Letter Fifty-Five

# Listen

Again Jesus said, "Peace be with you! As the Father has sent me, I am sending you." And with that he breathed on them and said, "Receive the Holy Spirit." ~John 20:21-22

# Reflect

My Beloved,

It's important to always remember that this life is not about you, but about me and my kingdom. Therefore, I am sending you. Since you have been seized by the power of my great affection, I am sending you into the world, just as the Father sent me, to be expressions of that life and love and delight.

So look at my life and see how I did it. Let that be the model and the foundation for all you do, as well as for how you do it. Go and make the word flesh; be visible expressions of the invisible God. Go and give your life away — love and serve. Become nothing, so that I might become everything. Become less, so that I might become more. Become hidden, so that I might become seen. Show this world who I am and how I love.

I know it sounds pretty overwhelming, but fear not, I have given you my Spirit. You do not go in your own strength, or by your own power, but you go on the winds of my breath.

So go now, my dear one. Go into this dark and lost and broken world, with the light and the hope and the love of the Father. Go because you love me, and want others to as well.

Love,
Jesus

# Respond

Write a letter to Jesus, telling him all that is in your heart.

# Letter Fifty-Six

# Listen

Now Thomas (called Didymus), one of the Twelve, was not with the disciples when Jesus came. So the other disciples told him, "We have seen the Lord!"

But he said to them, "Unless I see the nail marks in his hands and put my finger where the nails were, and put my hand into his side, I will not believe it."

A week later his disciples were in the house again, and Thomas was with them. Though the doors were locked, Jesus came and stood among them and said, "Peace be with you!" Then he said to Thomas, "Put your finger here, see my hands. Reach out your hand and put it in my side. Stop doubting and believe."

Thomas said to him, "My Lord and my God!" ~John 20:24-28

# Reflect

My Beloved,

When you begin to doubt the goodness of my heart, when you have a hard time convincing yourself of the depths of my love, and when you find that belief is waning in your weary soul, come and see, once again, the marks in my hands and the hole in my side. Make a regular practice of it. Put your finger where the nails were, and your hand where the spear pierced me. Then, stop doubting and believe.

Believe that I am the Risen One. Believe that I am bigger than death. Believe that you are worth dying for. Believe that you are fully and passionately and unconditionally loved.

Then you will be able to exclaim, as Thomas did, "My Lord and my God!" O fall in love with me, my Beloved.

Love,<br>
Jesus

## Respond

Write a letter to Jesus, telling him all that is in your heart.

# Letter Fifty-Seven

# Listen

Early in the morning, Jesus stood on the shore, but the disciples did not realize that it was Jesus.

He called out to them, "Friends, haven't you any fish?"

"No," they answered

He said, "Throw your net on the right side of the boat and you will find some." When they did, they were unable to haul the net in because of the large number of fish.

Then the disciple whom Jesus loved said to Peter, "It is the Lord!" As soon as Simon Peter heard him say this he wrapped his outer garment around him (for he had taken it off) and jumped into the water. The other disciples followed in the boat, towing the net full of fish, for they were not far from shore, about a hundred yards. When they landed, they saw a fire of burning coals there with fish on it, and some bread.

Jesus said to them, "Bring some of the fish you have caught."

Simon Peter climbed aboard and dragged the net ashore. It was full of large fish, 153, but even with so many the net was not torn. Jesus said to them, "Come and have breakfast," ~John 21:4-12

# Reflect

My Beloved,

I am with you always, even when you do not realize it. Even when you do not recognize me, I am still there. I know that sometimes life can get so busy, or so chaotic, or so painful, that it is hard to see anything but what's right in front of you. But rest assured, that does not mean I am not there, because I am. I am always with you, my Beloved. I am always thinking about you, always dreaming about you, always caring for you, always providing for you, always healing you, always at work in you, and always delighting in you, whether you are able to sense it or not. All you have to do is look up, or look around, or look within, and you will find me there.

I love you so much, my Beloved, and I simply cannot stay away from you. Just look for me in the events and experiences of your day and you will find me. Just listen for me in the voices within and around you, and you will hear my voice. I am with you always.

Love,<br>Jesus

## Respond

Write a letter to Jesus, telling him all that is in your heart.

# Letter Fifty-Eight

## Listen

When they had finished eating, Jesus said to Simon Peter, "Simon, son of John, do you truly love me more than these?"

"Yes, Lord," he said, "you know I love you."

Jesus said, "Feed my lambs."

Again Jesus said, "Simon, son of John, do you truly love me?"

He answered, "Yes Lord, you know I love you."

Jesus said, "Take care of my sheep."

The third time he said to him, "Simon, son of John, do you love me?"

Peter was hurt because Jesus asked him the third time, "Do you love me?" He said, "Lord, you know all things; you know I love you."

Jesus said, "Feed my sheep." ~John 21:15-17

## Reflect

My Beloved,

I love you more than life itself. I dreamt you into being and knit you together in your mother's womb. I formed your innermost parts with great care and intention, and I deeply love what I have made. When I think of you it brings a smile to my lips and joy to my heart. When I look at you my eyes light up and my heart leaps within me. How I long for you to know the depths and the fullness of my love. How I long for you to live your whole life from this deep inner reality, to know beyond a shadow of a doubt that you are my Beloved.

But I have to ask you this: Am I yours? Am I your Beloved? Do you love me with every fiber of your being? Do you love me more than life itself? Do you love me more than anyone or anything else in the world? Do you love me *more than these*?

If you do, then feed my lambs. It will be the natural result of loving me. Ministry is meant to be the result of the overflow of my life and love within you. But be careful, my Beloved, for if you don't love me *more than these* you will not feed my lambs, you will feed on my lambs. You will be so desperate for love and attention that you will extort it out of anyone and everyone who comes across your path. You see, you are only able to love because I first loved you. (1 John 4:19) And I do love you so much. My deepest hope is that you would fall more and more in love with me.

Love,<br>Jesus

## Respond

Write a letter to Jesus, telling him all that is in your heart.

# Letter Fifty-Nine

## Listen

"I tell you the truth, when you were younger you dressed yourself and went where you wanted; but when you are old you will stretch out your hands and someone else will dress you and lead you where you do not want to go." Jesus said this to indicate the kind of death by which Peter would glorify God. Then he said to him, "Follow me." ~John 21:18-19

## Reflect

My Beloved,

At times I am going to ask hard things of you, just as my Father asked hard things of me. Don't be surprised. The test of your love will be in whether or not you are willing to be led to places you would rather not go. Ultimately, Beloved, life with me is about *stretching out your hands* in trust and surrender. It is a life of submission and abandonment to my will and my direction, rather than clinging to your own. It is a life of following me wherever I lead, even if those places look hard, scary, and undesirable. You must always remember, Beloved, that this life is not about you, but about me. As you grow and mature, you will understand that more and more.

My deepest desire is that you reach the point where you love me so much that you are able to say, "Lord Jesus, I am willing to go wherever you want me to go and willing to do whatever you want me to do. I'll do anything for you." That's what it looks like when you truly fall in love with me.

Love,
Jesus

# Respond

Write a letter to Jesus, telling him all that is in your heart.

# Conclusion: Letter Sixty

# Listen

Jesus did many other miraculous signs in the presence of his disciples, which are not recorded in this book. But these are written that you may believe that Jesus is the Christ, the Son of God, and that by believing you may have life in his name. ~John 20:30-31

# Reflect

My Beloved,

I want life for you. And that life can only come about as a result of being totally and completely captured by my unbridled, passionate, extravagant, unfailing, and unconditional love. Because if you want to be a good lover, you must first learn how to be loved. Let me love you, and then let me love others through you; that's why I put you on earth in the first place.

It is my love that makes life worth living. It is my love that can truly satisfy your deepest longings. It is my love that can genuinely transform your life from what it is, into what I dreamt it to be. Which means that falling in love with me and staying in love with me are the most important things.

I hope these little letters have helped you to do just that. I hope you are more in love with me now than when we first began. For only when you have been seized by the power of my great affection, will all of your other affections be properly ordered.

I love you, my Beloved, never forget that.

Love,
Jesus

# Respond

Take a few minutes to reflect back over the course of our journey together. What has grown in you? What has God done? What has God said to you? How are you different now than when we began?

Now, go in peace to love and serve the Lord. Thanks be to God!

Made in the USA
Columbia, SC
01 November 2021